THE GOLDEN BOOK

FES – MEKNES
VOLUBILIS
MOULAY IDRIS – IFRANE

Text by
MOHAMED TEMSAMANI KHALLOUKI

Raimage
Raissouni Image

BB BONECHI

DISTRIBUTEUR POUR LE MAROC:

RAIMAGE SARL.
Angle Rues de Russie et Emsallah
Tél.934202, Tanger, Maroc

Project: Casa Editrice Bonechi
Project Manager: Monica Bonechi
Picture research, graphic design and cover: Serena de Leonardis
Make-up: Chiara Milano
Editing: Patrizia Fabbri
Text: Mohamed Temsamani Khallouki
Translation: Julia Weiss

© Copyright by Casa Editrice Bonechi - Firenze - Italia
e-mail: bonechi@bonechi.it - Internet: www.bonechi.it

Printed in Italy by Centro Stampa Editoriale Bonechi.

Photographs from the archives of Casa Editrice Bonechi *taken by* Marco
Bonechi *and* Andrea Pistolesi.

✳ ✳ ✳

Introduction

*F*ès and Meknès, the sister cities of the Sais plateau comprise a particularly significant social-urbanistic binomial. The traveler who is not thoroughly acquainted with the history and geography of this region in particular, and of Morocco in general, could be surprised by the location of these two large cities that are so close to each other. And yet, if we look at all the advantages inherent in this position, the explanation will seem quite obvious. In the first place, the entire area is of enormous strategic importance in controlling relationships and trade within Morocco as well as with neighboring countries. In fact, communications, in the east-west direction, between the Atlantic coast, eastern Morocco and the rest of the Maghrib make it almost a compulsory stop before entering the Taza corridor that crosses the Sais. Settling here, therefore means exercising a sort of right of control of all traffic, including trade, that always poured through this funnel-shaped area to reach the rich plains of the western region. It also has a similar importance in the organization of trade between the part of Morocco beyond the Atlas mountains and the Mediterranean coast as well as control of the Saharan trade routes that starting from Tafilalet or the Drâa Valley go towards the Mediterranean ports.

If all this were not sufficient, the position of Fès and Meknès is equally privileged because of the proximity of highly different areas. Majestic mountains, and green hills frame the entire plateau and supply its needs thanks to the forests and the development of many businesses: tree-raising in the areas before the Rif and livestock breeding on the Moyen Atlas. The plateau itself boasts more than insignificant resources. Located at an altitude of slightly more than 500 meters above sea level, and characterized by a slightly sloping landscape it has a good, moist climate while the soil's legendary fertility made it the bread-basket of Morocco. But if the grains grow readily, it is the olive groves that give this land a unique imprint. Their fruits yield a fine oil that is produced in the industrial plants of Fès and Meknès as well as in the many traditional presses that dot the region. Water is also abundant: the surface currents or underground springs are well regimented so that they can be used for many purposes. The entire plateau seems bounded or crossed by waterways that are essential for irrigating the fields and supplying the cities. In greater details, the Wadi Fès crosses the city of Fès, and the Wadi Bou Fekrane crosses Meknès. It is precisely because these two fluvial arteries reach into the hearts of the their respective cities that they have become the basis of social and economic activities. The water that gushes from the depths of the earth transformed the entire region into the main thermal basin of all Morocco. Moulay Yacoub, Sidi Harazem, Ain Allah, and Ain Shiffa offer enticing invitations to dedicate some time to health

and fitness. Moulay Yacoub and Sidi Harazem, in particular, located 22 and 10 kilometers from Fès, respectively, offer modern facilities with a wide range of services and treatments.

In historical terms, both Fès and Meknès were imperial cities, but their respective periods of glory varied considerably in duration. Fès was several times, and even relatively recently, the seat of central power. In any event, both cities are distinguished by centuries of history, and up to the colonial period were the main urban settlements and true driving forces in Morocco, basing their development on commerce and a strong network of contacts with the particularly rich inland zones.

Significant changes took place with the advent of the protectorate. As in other cities, the colonial authorities committed themselves to giving Fès and Meknès urban areas that could be considered European, and in both cases they developed at a due distance from the old town centers. Modern Fès was located on the Dar Debibagh plateau, while the new Meknès was built on the right bank of the Wadi Bou Fekrane. However, the conquering power soon showed itself capable of making much more fearsome changes. The development of the capitalistic production system with the industrial facilities that followed dealt a mortal blow to the traditional craft industries, bustling beehives of activity that for centuries had crowded the old cities. Furthermore, shifting the political and economic baricenters towards the Atlantic coast and designating Rabat as capital and Casablanca as the main port and the country's economic center deprived the old, inland imperial cities of their vital essence, so that entrepreneurs, capital and resources hurried towards the coast. These were major defections and their repercussions went beyond the economic and social spheres, making a strong impact on the urban fabric and the old historic nuclei that would soon decline due to a lack of means and also because they were subject to uses that had little to do with their true nature. This was soon followed by a massive influx of people: the farmers from the north were strongly lured by the two cities. It was a real migration that had two main consequences. First, the successive waves of this rural exodus that comprised the poorer part of the population, found the most appropriate refuge for their meager incomes in the medinas. The buildings suffered greatly: the old homes of the notables, built for a single family underwent transformations that irreparably comprised their habitability and the possibilities for proper maintenance. Umtamed divisions transformed the traditional middle class homes into real hovels that were crammed with numerous families. The second consequence was uncontrolled population growth that, in turn, broke the city into a nebula of suburbs that grew like mushrooms. Most of them were lacking even the most basic infrastructures, but were capable of hosting huge crowds. After a sort of truce, the city began to grow once more so that today the population of Meknès is about five hundred thousand, while Fès is well on the way to exceeding the one million mark.

Faced with the unstoppable degradation of the urban fabric of the old historic centers, more or less official initiatives and movements have been launched to sensitize public opinion about the need for safeguarding this priceless heritage. A huge mechanism has been put into action to save the medina of Fès that has been proclaimed part of the world heritage by UNESCO. In order to achieve the objective, a highly demanding project has been undertaken: to identify, analyze and take a census of the countless jewels in the old city in order to be able to launch appropriate recovery and salvage programs. The work, that began early in the nineteen eighties has made it possible to gather an enormous quantity of information about the treasures of the medina, while capillary surveys are being conducted on the old houses, palaces, madrasahs, and fondouks, the typical warehouse-homes. Recovery plans are being defined, and scenarios are being drawn up to restore new lymph and vitality to all those professional groups that are the true soul of these monuments and their sole guarantee of eternity. In this way, it has been possible to save them thanks to the contributions by the public authorities and private groups.

On the other hand, the two inland imperial cities have had to prove their incredible dynamism to guarantee themselves a better than secondary position in the context of the country's urban, economic and social development. Ambitious projects aim at creating infrastructures that facilitate communications with the ports and business centers along the coast, new industrial areas are being opened because, in parallel, but focusing on the transformation of traditional products and wares, the goal is also to guarantee the regional economy a solid base. Thus, while agricultural-food-

processing plants have been successfully operating in Meknès, textiles have been developing positively in Fès. And while Meknès obtained a university and hence a new role, the same role is being strengthened in Fès that is consolidating its official function as a city of the sciences and culture.

Finally, tourism, by virtue of the substantial flow of money it brings, is both encouraged and supported, and no one tires of emphasizing the considerable contribution that these two legendary cities can make to positive diversification of the Moroccan tourist offer. If the circuit of the imperial cities maintains its lure, it would be worthwhile to take action in order that the tourist roles of Fès and Meknès do not remain limited to this single sector. In this sense, Fès is certainly more dynamic, favored as it is by the traditional tour of the imperial cities that only includes a fleeting stop a Meknès. Furthermore, Fès is also helped by the recent development plans, which, have flanked the old luxury hotels (Palais Jamai, and Mérinides) with new jewels such as the Jnam Palace hotel complex. At the same, time efforts have been made to equip the city with entertainment and leisure facilities, such as the Golf Royal and create events that will help the world learn about and appreciate the Arab-Muslim cultural and historical heritage of which the city and its inhabitants are living repositories. One example is the "Festival of Sacred Music", which, already in its second edition has become an event of international scope and renown.

Tourists who venture into the medina alone love to walk and almost lose themselves in the streets that branch into little blind alleys, and in a moment of distraction, bump into mules or donkeys laden with modern goods that the consumer-oriented civilization insists on distributing to the inhabitants of the medina of Fès. The fact is that the medina, the Medieval part of the city, seems to be crystallized in a tight meshwork of a structure that dates from when it was first built, to when the protectorate imposed urban models and systems that were still unknown. And so, today, the medina seems besieged by buildings and businesses that gobble up the farmlands, raw materials and artisan wares.

It is indisputable that the two cities

could expect a better situation on the country's chessboard. Aside from the inestimable value of the cultural contribution they have made to the development of Moroccan civilization, the importance of their monumental arrangements and the architectural assets which are theirs alone, Fès and Meknès stand in midst of interesting elements and places that can enhance and diversify an already intriguing charm. Just a few kilometers from Meknès, for example, the ruins of Volubilis will take us back to ancient Rome, while near Fès, numerous springs provide an opportunity to soak in a fountain of youth after the crowd baths of the medina. And for those who prefer contact with nature? There is no problem, just 60 kilometers from here the Moyen Atlas offers wonderful fishing, hunting, skiing or merely invigorating walks through the splendid cedar woods, or along the shores of emerald green lakes that seem to be hidden in a treasure chest of plants or a basin of precious jewels.

FES
or the history of a glorious past

It was long believed that **Fès** was founded by Idris II, while historians and ancient writers agreed that the most likely date was 808. Then, in 1938 during the excavations in the heart of the city, the Oriental scholar, Lévi-Provençal found some silver coins, minted in Fès by Idris I, indisputable proof that the founder of the Idrisid dynasty was also the founder of Morocco's first imperial city. Actually, it would be more appropriate to speak of two different foundings, not too distant in time and essentially in the same place. Only the Wadi Fès created a physical separation between the two entities. Therefore, it was agreed that 789 would be considered the city's founding.

The choice went to the right bank of the Wadi Fès, where Berbers lived originally. Later, around 817 many refugees arrived from Cordoba, and they renamed the entire area *Adouat el-Andalous*, that is the "Andalusians' District". The second founding can be attributed to Idris II: in 809 he crossed the Wadi and created *Fès el-Aliya* that included an obvious reference to Alì, one of Mohammed's sons-in-law and ancestor of the founder. Later, with the arrival and settlement of many families of refugees from Tunisia and its then capital, Kairouan, the entire district was renamed *Qaraouiyyin*. In any event, this last settlement looked more like a city, with a *kaysaria*, the neighbor-hood reserved for artisans and merchants. Each of the two urban entities was surrounded by its own circle of walls, with gates. It was not, however, a mere topographic division: several chroniclers have written about the antagonism between the inhabitants of the two districts. It was no coincidence that when Idris II died, the two entities became autonomous, and each was governed by one of his grandsons.

In the latter half of the X century Ibn Hawqal visited the region and spoke of Fès as "an important city that a river divides in two, governed by two different emirs. Bloody and irresolvable conflicts erupt continuously between the populations of the two districts." It is widely agreed, however, that the city must have enjoyed a certain level of prosperity. Yacoubi wrote of "three thousand mills". And even Ibn Hawqal wrote of the abundance of "fruit, grains, foods, and goods...". Others wrote about the control of water resources and city maintenance "each day water from the river is let into the market, to wash the ground and cool the stones."

Thus, if history, but rarely succeeds in being truly objective, it is important to note that especially in the case of Fès it is elegantly filled with legend, and is accurate only in fabulous terms.

On the other hand, this argument that stimulates re-

Here and on the following pages: panoramic views of Fès that show the density of the urban fabric.

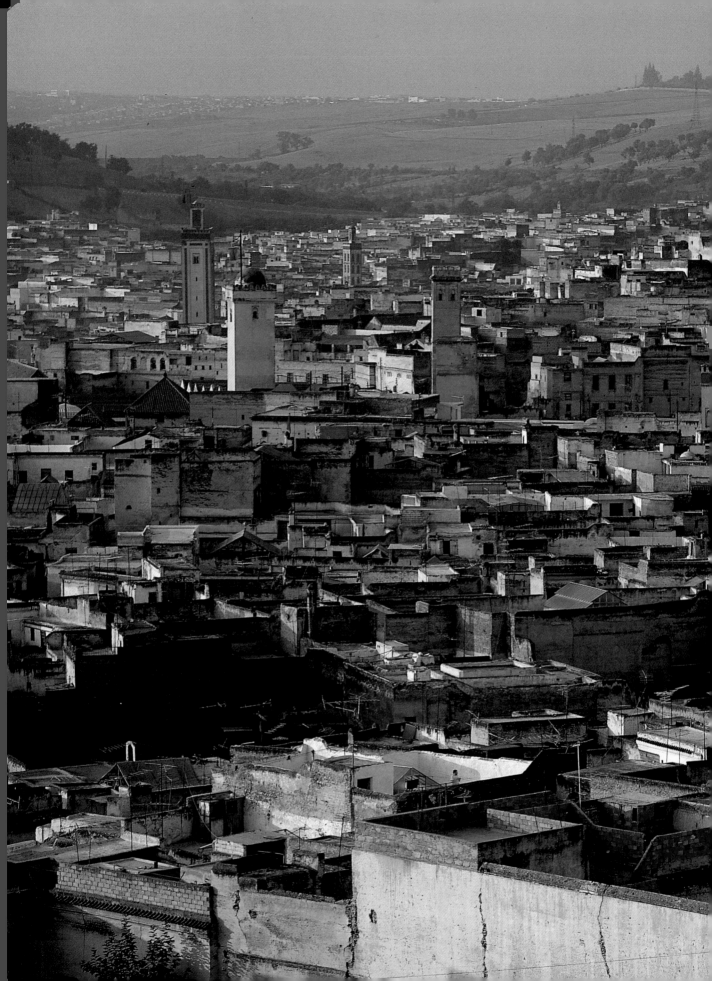

The splendid façade of Dar el-Makhzen, the Palace of the Government of the Sultan: the outstanding features are the refined decorations and elegant mosaics.

search and sharpens the analytical senses of archeologists, historians and scholars, matters little to the tourist or anyone who roams through the city. These people prefer to wander through the labyrinthine streets, the avenues that come to abrupt ends, the covered passageways and the infinitely winding little streets. Momentary visitors, these tourists gladly let themselves be swept along by the rivers of people that convey a strong sensation of true crowd baths.

The mutual isolation of the two districts ended with the Almoravid conquest. In 1069 Yusuf ibn Tashufin took over Fès and united it by enclosing the entire city within fortified bastions and tearing down the walls that separated the two districts.

If the city's situation appears essentially comprehensible, its location remains astounding. The basin, or depression, where the early settlements developed created significant obstacles to the expansion of the urban fabric since there are real escarpments to the north and south. The choice of the site, however, may be due to the fact that there was water since the area is crossed by three rivers, the Wadi Fès, the Wadi Zitoun and the Wadi Bou Kherareb, and there are many springs along their courses. In essence, it was the topography that imposed the way the city developed, and the best prospects have always opened to the west. Even the Marinids who began constructing the new city (*Fès el-Jédid*) in the XIII century had to deal with

these obstacles. They wanted to withdraw from the original site (*Fès el-Bali*), and above all, leave the basin for the plateau. The new settlement, that was called *El-Medinet el-Beida*, the "White City" became the official seat of royal power under the new dynasty. The new city was heavily fortified and abounded with palaces, mosques, and residential districts along with a *mellah*, the Jewish ghetto and a Christian suburb.

Even when, much later, under the colonial government, yet another new city was to be built, the western zone, with the Dar Debibagh to extend Fès el-Jédid, was once again the choice. Notwithstanding the construction of the new city, it was in Fès el-Bali that the Marinids erected the most beautiful buildings, especially mosques and madrasahs. In any event, all the dynasties, without exception wanted to contribute to the beautification and growth of Fès even at the end of the XIX century both sovereigns and the servants of power were committed to the urban rearrangement of some parts of the medina and to building palaces such as El M'nabhi and El Mokri for the vizier.

We have already seen how Idris II, who succeeded his father in 792, accepted approximately eight thousand refugees expelled from Cordoba in Andalusia, between 808 and 825, and nearly two thousand people from Kairouan who were fleeing from the menace of the Aghlabids, then lords of Tunisia. All these refugees, and a

11

Details of the façade of the royal palace and the rich, polychrome decorations of majolica tiles and mosaics.

mixed social group at that (they included Jews, Arabs and Christian converts to Islam) became the carriers of a refined civilization and considerable wealth, hastily subtracted from the armies of the *reconquista*. They had excellent general knowledge that was exceeded by extraordinary practical skills, among the most advanced of the period that proved capable of far-reaching influence. One of the main merits of this mixture was, without a doubt, that they were able to compact all the forces in Morocco at the time around a tolerant Islam, without which it would have been not only impossible, but also unimaginable to merge so many differences. We cannot overemphasize the benefits of tolerance and the primary role it plays in the flowering of the sciences, in the blossoming of the arts, in rooting faith, in cultural intermingling and in the development of trade in Fès. Ever since it was established the city was a prestigious center for science and trade, and it is thanks to this enormous prestige that reached beyond the borders of the country that it has managed to withstand the onslaughts of time, the vicissitudes of history and the appetites of the various dynasties that followed each other.

It became a famous tribune, and a compulsory passage for the dissemination of any new model of thought, ideological or scientific, spiritual or religious. Fès, quickly and deservingly earned the title of holy city and the role of irreplaceable leader in every field. After having national

*The inner courtyard of the Bou Inania Madrasah,
the basin and façades decorated with stucco work,
zellij and carved wood.*

importance as a century of legal, political and theological studies, it became a compulsory stop and a sort of elected homeland for each new dynasty attempting to conquer Morocco and power. Not even the French could escape its influence if it is true that they selected Fès as the site for signing the documents of the protectorate on 30 March 1912. And this is not all. Each dynasty, once it had achieved its goals, felt obligated to show itself superior to its predecessors on all levels, as a display of power and grandeur. This fascinating game, based on a "comparative proof" triggered a concurrence of circumstances favorable to the development of the city and its sphere of influence and Fès benefited enormously. The political-religious strength it achieved made it a "city-dynasty" in the heart of the Islamic west. Thus, it was able to escape from the sacking, raids and destruction which became all too familiar in other cities as a consequence of dynastic successions or foreign occupations.

Throughout the Middle Ages and the Renaissance Fès was the main center of learning and power in all Morocco. It was also, and above all, a place of writing, a ray of light in the immense darkness of the often blindly undertaken power struggles. Ever since it was established, around 789, the city had never abdicated its leading role in the scientific field, during a period in which obscurantist charlatans wore the robes of true knowledge. With its harmonious confusion Fès was able to conquer and charm inhabitants and occupiers alike, depriving the social-urban contradictions of their destabilizing components, creating a mix of constructive competition. This does not mean to say that there were no insurrections, but they were always subject to a sort of tacit agreement that maintained respect for religious institutions and works, that could not be matched anywhere else in the world. Thus, from the moment that all forms of destruction were prohibited, the various pretenders, once victorious could do nothing other than lure the people with projects, construction and creation, in a game of "popular charm" that reached its highest level under the reign of the Marinids. Their motto seemed to be "We must always do better to be able to convince better". It is exemplified in the places of worship, in the religious buildings and in the places for preaching in the residential districts as in the Turkish baths (places of purification) and in the artisans' workshops (places of creation). Even the forces whose duty it was to preserve law and order kept themselves at a distance, and stayed on the plateau where they could easily survey the city without provoking the populace. In the city, trade, the crafts, architecture and the arts prospered. With its famous mosque-university, el-Qaraouiyyin, its fascinating madrasahs, and richly decorated mausoleums, this agglomerate of countless mosques earned itself the role of a holy city during a period that Islam was still relatively young. In this way Fès

earned itself the institutional role of a place that was protected and a protector at the same time, where sacred and religious symbols and secular and material elements blended together to give life to a city in which wealth was based primarily on science and finance.

This was how Fès was created and how it managed to maintain an eternal image, of a city that is attractive and charming to visitors, scholars, craftsmen and Hispanic-Moorish and Islamic-Mediterranean merchants. Each and everyone could find what he was seeking since spiritual beliefs, religious teachings, artistic production, political considerations and material contributions had wisely succeeded in combining the concrete "here and now" with the spiritual "beyond". At that time, it was easy to become convinced that Fès, a true "Earthly Paradise" was nothing other than the antechamber to the "Heavenly Paradise". This impression led a Berber nomad who was visiting Fès one day to exclaim "May Allah allow the Fassi [the inhabitants of Fès] to enter Paradise, and my people of the Atlas mountains to enter Fès."

The door with the horseshoe arch and the richly decorated walls of the madrasah with many calligraphic inscriptions.

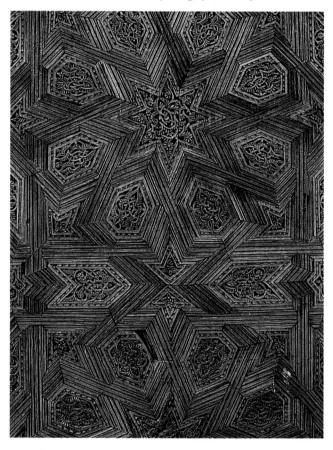

An unusual view of the clock facing the Bou Inania
Madrasah: its workings are still a mystery.

Fès, memory of the past, mirror of the present

In spite of vicissitudes linked to the passing of time, the city of Fès today is one of the most prestigious metropoles in the Arab-Muslim and Afro-Mediterranean world, a geographic and historic crossroads capable of challenging the simplistic chronicles and the reductive descriptions in the name of a history and of a legend that come together and enmesh perfectly in this place. One cannot go without the other. In a social and cultural context, such as the one we find in Fès, where history is richer than anywhere else in the Maghrib, the reliability of the facts and the chronicles of the events are marked by a precision and accuracy in which doubt can only be Cartesian. "No other city in the Maghrib appears as able to come to terms with time as Fès", affirms Jacques Berque. And nowhere else does time prove to be both and so exactly an enhancing factor and an agent that causes deterioration: even a rotten piece of cedar wood in a Marinid madrasah can seem marvelous; a block of *zellij*, the classic colored tile, that have seen dynasties, centuries and people come and go, has been capable of resisting all the trials of time; a column-capital, worn smooth by the years and by use, that boldly supports the weight of the building and of history, can confer an incal-culable historical and cultural dimension upon buildings, art objects and the artisans' districts of the medina. In this "living archeological site" that the tourist circuits have transformed into an authentic "open air museum", the monuments, the places, the historical objects have such a value that, in material terms, they are literally priceless.

If each city has its own peculiarities, a sort of special originality in relation to other urban centers, among the Muslim cities, the old town of Fès falls under the heading of exceptional. A growing Medieval village, over the centuries became a unique and united city in terms of space organization and urban management, cultural institutions, architecture and artistic production. It is an exceptional entity which, ever since its beginnings, had benefited from favorable circumstances with positive consequences.

To resist the perils of time and come down to our day, conserving an uncorrupted soul, in the purest tradition of Islamic art, the Medieval city, the result and perfect stratification of twelve centuries of progressive illumination on all occasions, including the battle for independence, faced dangers with the pen and preaching, with the book

The magnificent en-Nejjarin fountain, one of the oldest in Fès, dominates the square of the same name, with its myriad hued floral mosaic (left). On the left, the splendid entrance to the en-Mejjarin fondouk that probably dates from the XVIII century and is now a museum.

and prayer. By pouring rivers of ink it won amazing victories and extraordinary glory that were capable of lasting longer than those won with the sword that inevitably poured rivers of blood.

Fès, the most western city of the Muslim east has opened a new road to the European area of the Mediterranean, the Arab-Muslim world and the Afro-Berber reality, and through this pioneering role, rightfully earned an aura of nobility. Today it still seems suspended between popular legend and scholarly history, between the dream of the tourist and the reality of daily life.

Like the other great historical cities of our planet, Fès does not let her story be told easily, either orally or in writing. This leads to the necessity of combining pictures with the story in the hope of containing the deviationistic tendencies that are so typical of a reader's imagination. Anyone who crosses the Bab Boujeloud or reaches the Rif will find himself immersed in a historical-social context that can project him into a truly surprising past.

Narrow streets and blind alleys, houses and shops one on top of the other, old buildings, works of art and fabulous architecture, everything talks, with its age, its function and its appearance of Medieval Fès, of Islamic Renaissance Fès and of modern Fès. The optimum use of space, the artisan tradition, the mastery of manual labor have survived the onslaughts of time, the perils of history and the follies of man. They have come down through the centuries as messengers and witnesses of another era, uninterrupted temporal bonds, almost like an ideal bridge thrown between contemporary history and the distant

The Mausoleum of Moulay Idris, destination of Muslim pilgrims. Above, a detail of the Moulay Idris box for offerings.

past. A true challenge to modernization and to globalization, these activities are, in fact, the custodians and conservators of a significant part of the "historic past", ready to show it with pride today, as an exceptional result of the symbiosis of faith and law, polyvalence and tolerance, between science and awareness.

Resolute men or dreamers, seeking creative inspiration or concentrating on mastering their craft, the artisans repeat gestures that have come down through the centuries to perpetuate a thousand years of tradition. By so doing they also perpetuate functions that can take us back in time to the dawn of Islamic civilization. It was, actually, the contributions of many - Andalusians, Orientals, and natives - combined with favorable circumstances that generated the city's art and its crafts. Diversified yet homogeneous, everything took shape over the vestiges of ancient Roman art that had spread its roots as deeply as the heart of a Berber culture that was both eclectic and contemporary. Far from being an intriguing excursion or a tourist's walk through the ancient urban heart of the religious and cultural capital of the Kingdom of Morocco, a visit to the **medina** of Fès is, first of all, a leap back in time, into the history of the Medieval Muslim west.

Fès is one of those cities that never shows the same face

The entrance door with the horseshoe arch and the splendidly restored interior of the en-Nejjarin fondouk that arouses admiration for its subdued but elegant carved wood and stucco decorations.

A courtyard of the el-Attarin Madrasah.
The elaborate decorations alternate geometric motifs,
cursive script and elegant floral patterns.

to visitors, nor to the inhabitants who recently arrived from the Rif countryside and the Atlas Mountains. It is a city with its moods, its fortunes and also misfortunes. An authentic catalyst of Eastern and Western influences ever since its beginnings it has always been an attractive and alluring place because here wealth linked to trade and the artistic elegance of its building are inseparable. The urbanistic imprint, the architectural expressions and the artistic styles peculiar to the various dynasties that ruled in Fès are still clearly impressed in the mosque, the mausoleum, the madrasahs, the *fondouk* the typical warehouse that is both store and house, and in the classic middle class home.

Until quite recently the Idrisid city was the cradle of Islamic civilization, where the most fantastic and even some of the maddest ideas could be born, develop, be expressed and shaken: new ideas, freshly launched by unparalleled thinkers. For a long, or rather very long time,

and almost up to when the country achieved independence, Fès was the Maghrib tribune where all the sciences could develop and be perfected. It was the metropolis where power rose and inevitably fell. It was the geographic crossroads and historic relay station that sanctioned generations of exchange among scholars. It is as if to say that no new or rising power could have reasonably expected to govern at the national level if its main spokesmen had not been able to convince the prestigious community of scholars and creative thinkers in Fès with either words or deeds. Starting from the advent of the Idrisid kingdom, tradition demanded that each dynasty aspiring to political power was obliged to go to Fès and obtain the support of its notable citizens and the consent of its population as a final signal that they had, indeed, conquered. Here, popular consent and elite support had a price, a value and even a limit.

Historians, however, seem to agree that even when a dy-

Details of the decorations that embellish the inside walls of the el-Attarin Madrasah. The splendid capitals of the slim marble and alabaster columns are a source of admiration.

nasty left the city preferring to use another as capital, Fès continued to carry out its role as religious, economic and artistic capital, through to the first half of the twentieth century.

It was Marechal Lyautey, who transferred the capital to Rabat in 1929 and created a new economic center in Casablanca, causing and sanctioning the temporary decline of Fès. But Fès took revenge in its own way, and in the early 'fifties, became the standard-bearer of the resistance in the struggle for independence.

Today, the Idrisid city is famous for its rich history rather than its current political and social role. This, however, does not prevent it from being in the front lines along with the more influential cities of the kingdom. And, even if it is arguable whether Fès has truly been able to withstand the attacks of time and history, it is no less true that today it struggling to deal with the violence it has suffered, starting from the economic and social decline, sad consequences of the imposition of a way of life and economic system that are but poorly compatible with its ancient structures and organization. Restaurants, cafés, hotels, built in the old middle-class homes, in the old heart of the city try to obtain clients and the modern facilities that require space and speed, two elements that

A close-up view makes it possible to appreciate the skills that went into these decorations, that combine calligraphy and geometric motifs to form arabesques worthy of an elegant fabric.

On the following pages: the majestic courtyard of the el-Qaraouiyyin Mosque, one of the largest in the entire Maghrib, with the traditional pool for ablutions.

have never been very important in the medina of Fès. It is a context in which self-confidence and indolence, active participation and a thoughtful attitude cohabit normally, without difficulties.

The city's position offers the visitor the incredible advantage of being able to see the entire complex of the medina in a single glance. The hills surrounding the city offer perfect observation points to acquire a bit of familiarity with its features before venturing into the little streets of the medina. It would be best to start a familiarization tour of Fès by walking around the city on the outer roads. In a few hours you can get a good idea of the size of the inhabited district by evaluating the power of the bastions that protect it, see the main access roads and discover - with almost perpendicular perspectives - the complexity, compactness and, in some ways, the historic opacity of the Muslim city that we will then visit more thoroughly.

The itinerary starts at Place de la Résistance in the modern city and requires an automobile because it covers approximately 15 kilometers. We will go to the valley of the

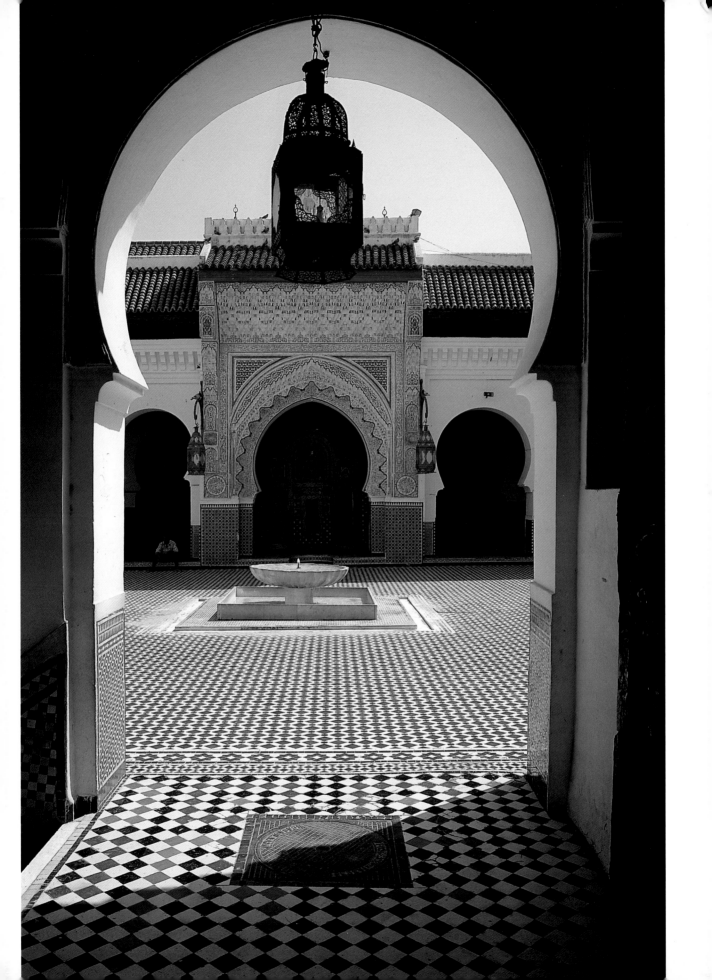

The richly decorated interior of the es-Sahrij Madrasah, known also as the School of the Pool, because of the large pool in the center of the courtyard.

Wadi Zitoun, and travel along it as far as the **Bab Ftouh** cemetery, one of the main access gates to the medina. From here a road to the right goes uphill to a building known as **Borj Sud**. It is a fortress built in the XVI century during the Sa'di domination, and it was probably meant to keep the inhabitants of Fès at bay. Today it is of interest solely because it offers a view of the entire city and a panorama that extends to Fès el-Bali, a stratification of endless terraces hugging the hillside. The religious buildings stand out because of their sloping, green tiled roofs, minarets and domes. On the right are the minarets of the two twin mosques, el-Qaraouiyyin and the Mosque of the Andalusians, that offer the observer a useful reference point. The impressive size of the el-Qaraouiyyin Mosque along with the Mausoleum of Moulay Idris mark the middle of the urban area. At the hour of the prayers it is truly moving to hear the cries of the *muezzin* from all the minarets. From this point we can even see a good part of the bastions with the monumental Bab Ftouh gate and the **cemetery** of the same name where nearly all the *ouléma*, the learned theologians who taught in the el-Qaraouiyyin Mosque now rest. And, then farther beyond, within the walls, we see the **Zaouia of Sidi Alì Boughaleb**, a theater of frenetic activity on the occasion of each *mouloud*, the holiday commemorating the birth of a saint, when the city's barbers pay tribute to their patron, and circumcise the sons of the poorer families.

Today, there is a recovery project underway aimed at restoring proper dignity to this area where the remains of so many men of science rest. There is a plan to build a library to honor the erudition of all these *fouqaha*, the wise men who, through the centuries, drew legions of men who thirsted for knowledge, from all over the world, to the university.

A "sound and light" performance now permits an impressive reconstruction of the city's history. It is a clever blend of words, music, and above all lights which, in 45 minutes makes it possible to admire the principal monuments of Fès as they are illuminated against the darkness of the night.

Now we will come to what could be considered a ring-road, and we will drive along the walls. After a few kilometers we will come to the monumental entrance to the **Hotel Palais Jamai**, located in the old palace that, at the end of the nineteenth century, belonged to the vizier Sidi Mohammed el-Jamai. Then, we will come to the hill of **el-Kolla**, with the Marinid necropolis. This promontory offers a far-reaching view, especially on the right where it extends to Fès el-Jédid and part of the modern city. Continuing our tour we will come to the second Sa'di fortification, **Borj Nord** which is also the home of the **Weapons Museum**. If we continue along the walls as far as the road to Meknès and Rabat, we can go left to Fès el-Jédid.

The lively artistic crafts

There has always been a deep bond between the religious buildings and the places dedicated to crafts production and trade. At the prayer hour, those who were in the shops could use a special entrance to the places of worship. This co-presence also has an economic and practical significance. In fact, the upkeep of the religious buildings was made possible thanks to the rents for the various workshops and stores. In truth, all the sovereigns or private citizens who financed the construction of the mosques and madrasahs created a group of mortmain assets that would guarantee the money for proper building maintenance and the caretakers' salaries. If the income was sufficient the money could also be used to help finance the management of the entire city. In fact, in what is the main nucleus of the old settlement we can see how the areas destined for multiple purposes intermesh; in addition, it was also a great privilege to be able to live near the great mosque. Whether it was science or trade, the main activities concentrated around the central node represented by the el-Qaraouiyyin Mosque and the Mausoleum of Moulay Idris. There are three madrasahs within a radius of 200 meters of this center: **el-Attarin**, **ech-Cherratin** and **es-Seffarin**. Their names are obvious references to the trade groups to which they were reserved: the grocers, the rope makers and the brass workers.

The members of these trades organized themselves in different ways as far as space was concerned. Sometimes their shops would be in a straight row along an entire street, or they could be grouped around a square, or within areas well-defined by doors that were closed in the evenings. In some cases the artisans established themselves in buildings specially built for their businesses such as the *fondouk* **en-Nejjarin**. One whole district was reserved for the carpenters-cabinetmakers as proof of the importance of woodworking, especially the fine cedar that comes from the forests of the Moyen Atlas.

Thus, in a single space we find Place en-Nejjarin (the carpenters' square), the en-Mejjarin *souk*, the en-Nejjarin *fondouk* and the fountain of the same name. The entire complex was restored recently. Thanks to donations by private parties we can now speak of a true rebirth of the district that has been restored to its original function, and an appropriate place within the context of the medina.

The streets and squares of Fès are always crowded, even near the Mosque of the Andalusians that has a majestic portal.

A typical scene in the dyers' and tanners' district.

Left, one of the elaborate windows of the Mosque of the Andalusians.

This great project, conducted by the ADER-Fès, was able to mobilize the best of the city's powers that were convinced of a need to infuse new lymph into a craft that had made one of the greatest contributions to the development and dissemination of the artistic skills of the inhabitants of Fès. There is not a single monument in the city that does not bear some signs of these craftsmen's skills. They have an artistic ability that has proved itself in the restoration of the *fondouk*, since many master craftsmen (*maalem*) also participated in the project. Another significant innovation concerns the *fondouk* itself, it has been transformed into a museum of the crafts and trades related to woodworking. Periodic exhibits illustrate the contributions of the craftsmen of Fès to the development of this specific sector and the various contexts in which they work: making tools and furniture and even real architecture. This initiative will certainly guarantee a new dynamism to this trade with the promotion of the woodworking crafts, and a strong stimulus for its propagation, the only vehicle that can guarantee a long future.

Similar programs should be undertaken for the other artistic crafts in order to guarantee the vitality of the Fès artisans who deserve the credit for having made the monumental heart of the city famous throughout the world.
All around the el-Qaraouiyyin Mosque is a bustling beehive of activity: and this is, in fact, the true essence of any visit to the medina. Beyond the purely architectural and urbanistic aspects, it is the meeting with the craftsman at work in his shop and observing the skills of the *maalem* engrossed in the exact moment that they create a work of art that most fascinates the visitor. It is impossible to remain insensitive when watching this beehive where the work of each individual contributes to perfecting the work of all. Those who took the responsibility for protecting the medina of Fès were entirely right in insisting that the city's artistic activities be guaranteed all the support necessary for their survival and development. Only by properly exploiting the vital force of these micro-entrepreneurs will the medina be able to guarantee itself full mainstreaming into the city's life, by representing one

The many vats used for tanning and dyeing hides that characterize the tanners' district and souk. The tanners work in these unhealthy conditions from dawn to dusk.

of its most dynamic focal points. Making Fès el-Bali an area for living, working and creativity rather than a sad museum of lamentations is a big wager and it will soon be won.

The various trades are also offering a certain amount of resistance to the systematic aggression to which all the artistic crafts have been subject. Organized in guilds they have maintained the cohesion that permitted their crafts to survive through the centuries, handed down from generation to generation. Each of the craft activities is headed by master craftsmen or *maalem* who work with the help of one or more *metaalem*, and the apprentices complete the group. The *maalem*'s working companions can, in turn, become master craftsmen after they have attained a certain level of perfection and obtained the consent of their master. Each guild is governed by strict rules to guarantee the seriousness and survival of the craft. The *amin* is elected by his peers in his guild and has to monitor the entire category's work. It is also he who settles disputes that may arise among the craftsmen and propose solutions to misunderstandings that may occur with

Bab Boujeloud, with its crenellations leads into the medina. The towering minarets can be seen through the horseshoe arch.

clients. In addition to his role as a judge, the *amin* directly manages the social affairs of his guild and oversees the preparations for the events in which the craftsmen are invited to participate. They are also the driving force behind the *moussem* the yearly pilgrimage undertaken to express gratitude to the patron saint of the city.

The *moussem of Moulay Idris el-Azhar*, is one of the main festivals in Fès, it lasts for a week and is marked by processions of Fassi who bring offerings. At this time it is traditional to renew the *kssaoua* (the cloth) that covers the catafalque of the tomb, and the city's artisans are the ones who make the new *kssaoua*. The procession is a very colorful sight.

As we have said, the working areas are arranged in specific agglomerates of individual entities engaged in the same functions. Generally, we will see places dedicated to production and areas for trade. However, it is rather usual for an artisan to sell his own wares, or for the workshops to be right next to the stores. We will remain in this central area that offers a wide range of activities (artistic crafts, trade, etc.) grouped in different ways: *kaysarie*, *souks* and shops line the streets or larger areas such as the

The medina of Fès a meshwork of narrow, crowded and winding streets teeming with craftsmen, shops and blind alleys.

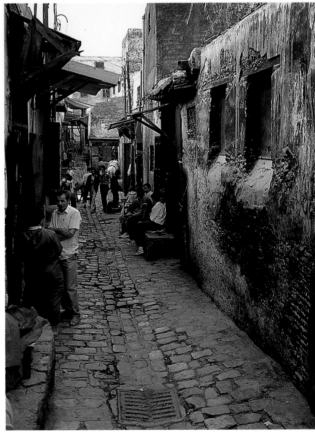

tanners' district or the older, potters' neighborhood. Our visit will begin at the **souk** of the **henna**.

Next to the Mausoleum of Moulay Idris the souk offers such a wide range of choices that it is one of the most highly visited places. Even though it has given its name to the entire *souk*, henna, the widely used dye, is not the absolute protagonist since this market has specialized in natural substances for body care. Here we will find all kinds of beauty products, from *kohl*, the Oriental eye-shadow, to

From the brass workers to the potters, from the cabinet makers to the spice sellers, you can meet many interesting people in the souks and the streets of the medina where mules and donkeys are still the main form of transportation.

perfumes, to *ghassoul*, a clay with a distinctive odor that is ideal for the bath. Some shops also offer a fine assortment of terra-cotta wares.

Not far, after passing by the Mausoleum of Moulay Idris we will come to another, no less lively *souk*, the *souk* **Chemmaine**; the name evokes the original specialty of this market, waxes. Currently it is the place to shop for bridal trousseaus. Beautiful embroidered belts hang in the windows, but it is mainly the dried fruits, enormous quantities in large bins arranged on the counters, attract our attention: almonds, hazelnuts, dates of all varieties are there to be tasted while the merchant, with a wink, praises their energy giving and aphrodisiac qualities. As to **el-Attarin**, the only possible, and rather simplistic, translation is "grocers". This is the grocers' street par excellence, a central road that benefits from the two main places of worship in the medina and the junction of the two main roads of Fès el-Bali. No matter where you enter the medina, your will inevitably come to the el-Attarin *souk*. The market is quite linear, with a long row of shops and counters with artisans and merchants next to each other. Here you can buy clothing and shoes, or spices or

merely let go in the symphony of colors or fantasies of the distant countries where these magical goods with their unmistakable fragrances originate. The **kaysaria** is the main business center of the medina, we reach it from Rue el-Attarin. We will see many goods that are important to the people of the medina, and of the city in general: clothing, babouches, jewelry and silks abound. Every evening the gates to the *kaysaria* are closed with chains and they are guarded by the *Oulad sidi Issa* who also carry merchandise and messages throughout the medina.

The artisans' work adds its own dimension of sound to the many colors and odors; when we come to Place es-Seffarine it will be obvious. A whole range of sounds will welcome us, from the heavy hammer blows of the tinkers, to the sharp clatter of the brass workers' punches on copper plates. The square is a melee of copper and brass utensils, tools and echoing hammers. Huge cauldrons set on the ground wait to be bought for a wedding. Further along we come to the dyers' street. Here the work is quieter, but the colors are just as lively. Freshly dyed skeins of wool hang like stalactites.

The scene and the dimensions of the tanners' district are quite different. But what is the most striking aspect, the organization, the profusion of colors, the clinging odors or the working conditions of these craftsmen? The least we can say is that we must acknowledge the merits of these tanners who stand in chemical-filled vats all day, stamping the hides. The process is long as we can see from the huge number of pits and basins that dot the ground. It takes many treatments and process to make a piece of leather. Pigeon guano, lime, alum and tannin are just a few of the substances in which the hides must macerate. The enormous use of pollutants that the process requires have raised the issue of transferring the tanneries outside the medina to a critical level.

Zellij! is a word with a magical sound. In any event, the work of these artisans who make these typical tiles, has always brought sunshine to the places where their panels and tiles are used. Each composition sparkles with a thousand colors, like a rose window; each one seems to release the warmth they absorb during firing. After this "baptism-by-fire" the smooth, shiny glaze will never change.

The raw material, clay, comes from nearby. After it is quarried, the large blocks are broken up and placed into vats where they are impregnated with water. Once the clay is friable, it is worked until it is malleable and shaped into blocks measuring 15 cm on a side. When the

The potters making vases and bowls: one of the most fascinating sights of the Fassi crafts.

blocks have attained a certain consistency, they are compacted by hand and pressed into 10 cm square tiles. Then they are fired for the first time. The procedures for glazing and defining the colors are absolute secrets. Each *maalem* has his own technique for creating the structure and brilliance of the enamel. A second, and final firing fixes the colors the colors for eternity, like those that have been glimmering on the walls of the el-Qaraouiyyin Mosque for over one thousand years.

There are two techniques used to make the *zellij* panels. The first, that is applied to already cut tiles, uses the entire surface: the portion of the pattern is traced onto it. Then the *maalem* scratch the enamel so that the patterns, often inscriptions or floral motifs, are raised. Combinations of different tiles create the friezes or panels like those that decorate public buildings, religious monuments and private homes. The second technique is somewhat more complex. The master craftsman (*maalem naquach*) creates and traces the patterns onto the tiles.

Then they are copied and the required number of pieces are cut. All the steps are done by hand, proof of the craftsmen's consummate skill as they create over two hundred different patterns, so small as to further confirm their abilities. Once these tiles are placed in groups the patterns contribute to the magnificence of the interiors of the madrasahs and palaces.

The ceramics of Fès, and mainly the plates, have been famous since the X century. As varied as they are, the shapes and decorations follow very precise rules. Textiles are also part of the city's finest craft products.

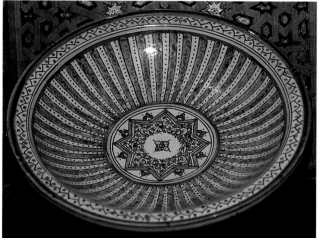

Spices and fruits, jewels and pottery, mirrors and metal wares of all shapes and sizes enliven the crowded, picturesque souk of Fès.

Bab Segma, one of the gates on the outermost walls, crowned with crenellations and the arch inscribed in the subtly decorated rectangle.

The origins of the university: the madrasahs

The Marinids were the first to introduce the **madrasah,** the Islamic institute of higher learning, into the socio-cultural panorama of Fès and into the socio-political life of Morocco. The first madrasah, that has been documented dates from the XIII century. The idea of building a madrasah in Fès came from the sultan Abou Yusuf, one of the first sovereigns of the Marinid dynasty. His successors built others and rivaled each other in the artistic decorations that were based primarily on carved cedar wood, decorative stucco work and graffito majolica. Thus, in a short time the madrasahs were transformed into masterpieces of Islamic architecture during the Marinid era.

The madrasah, that originated in Persia, is a sort of school of theology that provides room and board. The founding sultan covered all the expenses to build it, while management costs, including the teachers' salaries and the costs for keeping and teaching the students came mainly from the income from the *habous*, bequests to religious institutions. Donations from the wealthier families of Fès were used to cover the costs of building maintenance and to support the poorer students.

This was a wonderful initiative on the part of the Marinids: as opposed to the classic Koranich schools, the madrasah guaranteed a high level of education under qualified supervision. Here the future *ouléma*, learned theologians, were taught the political ideology and religious doctrine allowed by the authorities in power. The dynasty was concerned about how its image and prestige were conveyed to its future servants.

As the years went by, a classic architectural model gradually developed for the madrasah. The building stands around a square, or slightly rectangular, carefully paved patio. In the middle there is a fountain with a basin or pool carved from a block of marble. The arrangement is essentially the same in each madrasah. On the ground

floor, one side of the patio leads to a large prayer room, while the other three open onto classrooms that hold from 10 to 15 students. Finely carved wooden grilles, known as *moucharabieh* form the doors to the classrooms, while the fretwork windows are placed high enough to prevent the curious from looking in and distracting the students.

The reason that the decorations in the prayer rooms are usually subdued is probably to help the faithful concentrate.

Baths and sanitary facilities are usually situated in isolated corners or outside the main rooms, for privacy and to keep away odors, especially in summer when water flow is quite reduced.

The decorations on the walls facing the internal courtyard are incredibly beautiful. It is easy to distinguish three bands of patterns. In the lowest band, on the ground floor, reaching from the ground to a height of about 2 meters, polychrome tiles form a shining and sturdy wall covering; the second band is chiseled plaster that is painted to a large extent. It covers a significant area that reaches the base of the roof, supported by finely carved cedar wood corbels. These roofs, covered with green tiles serve a dual purpose, in addition to being decorative, they provide protection as they allow the rain water to run off far from the decorated walls.

If we look around a full 360° at the walls of the internal courtyard of a madrasah, we will be struck by the clever and perfect use of the arch - in all its possible variations: from the simple or multifoiled horseshoe, to the lambrequin arch with stalactites, to the broken horseshoe with alveoli. The shapes and decorations demand admiration, and it is difficult indeed to remain untouched by power of these marvels.

Inscriptions in Kufic or cursive script present verses from the Koran and the laws of Allah. Often these friezes contain praises of the sultan who founded the madrasah, even if there is already a commemorative plaque, celebrating his deeds and powers, at the entrance.

Kufic writing (from Kufa in Iraq) is the oldest form, and consists of pointed, rather sparse characters. It is, rather, the cursive form that we see most frequently throughout the Maghrib and Andalusia, and there are three different styles of cursive: Neskhi, Thoulthi and Andalusian.

In all Morocco there are about a dozen madrasahs (in Marrakech, Salé and Meknès), and seven are in Fès. The oldest is the **es-Seffarin Madrasah**, located near the famous el-Qaraouiyyin Mosque. Its name comes from the square of the brass workers (*seffarin* in Arabic), that provides the access. This madrasah, that was remodeled and restored several times has lost much of its original features.

Little or nothing remains of the second madrasah that was built in Fès el-Jédid by Abou Said in 1320, since it was replaced by a smaller one in the eighteenth century. In 1321 when there was still but little of the madrasah begun by Abou Said in Fès el-Jédid, his son, Abou el-Hassan began construction of the **es-Sahrij Madrasah**. A third, much smaller madrasah, **Sebaiyine** was built later. We can safely say that Marinid art reached its apex with the construction of the es-Sahrij Madrasah where everything is harmony, virtuosity and perfection. The artisans who created this masterpiece succeeded fully in conferring the highest level of nobility on carved cedar wood.

Father and son continued their rivalry in building madrasahs, with great benefits for the arts and education. In 1323 Abou Said began building what can rightly be considered the most beautiful madrasah in Fès and all Morocco. In fact, the **el-Attarin Madrasah** is innovative in both decoration and concept. It offers the visitor one of the most interesting and beautiful galleries of decorative plaster work and leaded glass.

The **Misbahiya** that is named for Féquih Misbah, who was in charge of the works stands, like all the others except for the one in Fès el-Jédid, in the el-Qaraouiyyin district. The unstable ground, the loads imposed by the wooden structures and nearby works led to infiltrations that compromised the stability of the building. This, in turn required major work to consolidate the complex at the expense of modifying its original features. Fortunately, thanks to the direct intervention of the king, the work needed to save this authentic jewel of Arab-Muslim architecture has already begun.

The **Bou Inania Madrasah** on the other hand, has survived through the centuries nearly intact. And, current restoration work that is respectful of the building's artistic spirit and history will guarantee further consolidation so that it may be truly restored to its ancient splendor. It took five years (1351-1356) and enormous sums in the Middle Ages to build this masterpiece. The costs were covered by the Fès community and its subject provinces. Tradition tells us that the final figure was enormous, but when the grand vizier submitted the list of expenses to Abou Inan, the ruler pushed it away and said "What is beautiful is never expensive no matter what the price and no one can ever pay too much for something that pleases him."

The real innovation in this madrasah was a clock with thirteen gongs that were operated by an extremely clever hydraulic system. Even today, it challenges modern technology since no one has yet been able to understand the mechanism or how this Marinid clock actually worked. There is, however, a rumor that quite recently an engineer has finally discovered the complicated secret.

Ever since its beginnings Fès has reserved a special place in its socio-urbanistic development for the **mosque**, the place where Muslims gather for prayer five times a day. As opposed to the madrasah, the mosque need not have a central courtyard; but, then it will have high windows, to let in light to preserve the intimate atmosphere inside for the faithful. The room for prayers has naves, marked off by pilasters or columns. The main nave leads to the *mihrad*, a niche for the *imam* who leads the prayers. Near the *mihrab* is the *minbar* a pulpit for sermons, it is usually made of more or less elaborately carved cedar wood.

The mosque is topped by the minaret, a high tower that will allow the *muezzin's* voice to carry far as he calls the faithful to prayer. The height and shape of the minarets vary from mosque to mosque: the most common shape is a square, while the hexagonal (the Chechaouen medina) and octagonal (the casbah in Tangier) forms are extremely rare.

The oldest and largest mosque in Fès is the **el-Qaraouiyyin** with its fourteen doors, sixteen naves and two hundred and seventy columns. Established in 857 by Fatima ben Mohammed el-Feheri, a native of Kairouan - from which the building gets its name - and sister to the woman who ordered the oratory that would later become the Mosque of the Andalusians, el-Qaraouiyyin is a true

The majestic ruins of the Marinid necropolis on top of the el-Kolla hill that overlooks the city.

jewel of religious architecture. The original building was enlarged and remodeled several times; the most important expansions were done in 933 and 1135. Its role as a university (theological sciences) dates from the X century as does the minaret that was built in 956. Among the many artistic marvels that we can admire inside, the two marble columned kiosks, the elegant *moucharabieh* panels and a chandelier datable around 1203, that is the era of the Almohadi, deserve special mention.

El-Qaraouiyyin is the seat of the Muslim University of Fès, it has a wonderful *library* that contains 30,000 volumes, nearly 10,000 are which are manuscripts.

A bird's eye view of Meknès.

MEKNES

If, from all standpoints, Fès is the unrivaled first of the imperial cities, **Meknès** is the youngest (XVII century) and smallest sibling. Part of the tour of the imperial cities, it is rich in attractions, both because of its role as a crossroads and because of its unusual monuments. It is called "Ismailia capital" and the name is extremely appropriate: a tribute to Moulay Ismail, a contemporary of Louis XIV who wanted the capital of his kingdom to be at the geographic crossroads of the north-south, and east-west routes. Meknès is also an important regional metropolis that cannot be overlooked, as well as a fortified town of considerable historic importance.

Meknès is often presented as a copy of Versailles on Islamic soil, built of *pisé* the construction material made of clay, stones and straw. It is also said that Moulay Ismail, a contemporary and friend of Louis XIV was very impressed by the descriptions and sketches his ambassador Ben Aicha brought back from Paris after a diplomatic visit. In any event, it is important to remember that the construction of the imperial city was actually begun long before the 'Alawi sovereign learned about Versailles. In essence, this city is a unique experience if for nothing other than its size. However, Meknès can also be considered unique in its general urban layout: a succession of walled corridors and open squares, for its austere archi-

tectural style that, although favoring, beaten earth, is not lacking in highly refined sections, and finally for its function as a defensive military complex built entirely of *pisé*. The imperial city can rightfully be considered an inhabited center, a palace and a military fort. Moulay Ismail, the first of all the sovereigns of the various dynasties that ruled Morocco wanted to create a clear separation - that was quite difficult for those times - between the religious (Fès) and the political (Meknès). It was mainly because he faced the religious power represented by the *ouléma* (Islamic scholars and theologians) of Fès that the second king of the 'Alawi dynasty resolved to create a distance between the social clerical-elite binomial of Fès and his capital.

During the fifty-five years of his reign, Moulay Ismail extended his power throughout Morocco; he created relationships and established contacts with the Western European kingdoms; he drove the Spanish and Portuguese invaders from the northwestern coast of his country and released Tangier from the English domination. He did not hesitate in using foreign prisoners, especially if they had special knowledge, in town planning, architecture and building, to make their stays profitable for Meknès and earning their freedom more likely.

On the other hand, if the establishment of the imperial

city brought Meknès permanent fame, the origins of the settlement date back to the X century, and perhaps even earlier if we want to give credence to certain historians. The first urban agglomerate could be dated around the year one thousand. In the X century a Zenata tribe from the east, struck by the fertility of the plain of Sais, and after have been around the famous city of Fès - which was certainly too refined for a group of nomads - preferred to settle at a reasonable distance so that they could enjoy its benefits without trouble, and also to be able to watch it without giving rise to provocations.

Later, between the XV and XVI century the city declined markedly, and had to wait for the advent of Moulay Ismail who promoted its rebirth. Probably he was prompted to select this place as the base for extending his power throughout Morocco by the same considerations that determined the choice of the Zenata tribe. Thus the village of **Meknès ez-Zeitoun** "Meknès of the olive trees" awoke from its lethargy and rose to the rank of a great capital. But what sort of capital was it? It was a mighty capital yet distinguished by a fleeting life: about half a century of an imperial existence. Upon the death of Moulay Ismail, in 1727, the imperial nature of the city, its power, its brightness and its influence proved incapable of surviving the loss of its founder. The struggles for the succession ended up by compromising from within the future of a kingdom that seemed to have settled all its problems. It was a dream apparently destined to remain unfulfilled.

"During the course of the centuries, the monuments of the imperial city became symbols of resistance to the vicissitudes of history and the onslaughts of time, in the image of the founder, Moulay Ismail who was able to overcome difficulties and obstacles and to challenge all the historical chronicles with his long reign and daring achievements. The royal city, with its clay buildings and architecture that combined audacity and sobriety, quantity and quality, esthetics and functionality, is an outstand-

At the entrance to the tomb of Moulay Ismail you can still encounter one of the most typical characters on the Moroccan scene: the water seller.

The elegant courtyard Mausoleum of Moulay Ismail.
The beautiful ceiling (above) of the room that leads
into the funeral chamber, covered with painted, carved
cedar wood, stands out in a maze of doors and hallways.

ing lesson in living history, providing an excellent opportunity for those who love and admire brilliant art. In any event only those with penetrating tastes that are sensitive to the different, with sharp eyes and a particularly strong spirit of observation will go into ecstasy as they visit the ruins, the bastions and historic buildings. The imperial city, with its unique monuments (imperial palaces, religious buildings and *pisé* military bastions) offer something truly sensational for those who know how to see and perceive. If the educated and merely curious person can be content with the explanations of a well-informed, skilled guide who is capable of explaining art, and if the less educated visitor is astonished by the approximations of a young school-dropout who becomes a self-styled guide, the scholar will almost always remain dissatisfied in spite of the commitment and unequaled competence of an official guide.

This city, with its powerful walls, massive gates, decorated archways, pyramidal domes and endless corridors seems to hold treasures, secrets and conceal all sorts of mysteries. Its architectural heritage and its urban structure belong to the category of 'easy-inaccessible and simple-inimitable'. This feature led the English historian Braitwaite to state that the buildings of Moulay Ismail 'can be viewed more as a city rather a palace'. Historic reference point and geographic crossroads of Morocco,

The majestic outer courtyard of the Mausoleum of Moulay Ismail is decorated with colored ceramics.

Meknès as something more than the other imperial cities: Berber-Roman before it opened up to the Arab-Islamic culture, with Tangier it was the first city to establish contacts with Europe and open its doors to Judeo-Christian culture.

If the other cities of the *makhzen*, the seats of power, owe their fame to the advent and succession of the various dynasties and the passage of centuries, for the imperial city of Meknès half a century and a single sovereign were sufficient to make it part of history. A single man and a short period of time sufficed to bestow nobility upon this region and its history. Alas, however, aside from agriculture and its offshoots (trade and food-processing) one of Meknès's fortes, that is, tourism, is overshadowed by its imperial sisters, Fès, Marrakech and Rabat - not to mention names. Is it possible that because of its agricultural potential Meknès has been victimized as far as tourism goes? Indeed yes! 'Princess of the olive trees', writes Michel Jobert, 'does not know the illusion. Guileless peasant girl, artist by application, only he who loves her

The basin of Agdal and the adjacent cisterns, flanked by the enormous stables, guaranteed the city sufficient reserves of water.

can understand her, and that is all she cares about.' And it is precisely this that yields nearly nothing insofar as tourism is concerned. Everything, apparently, lead us to believe that the established hierarchy and stereotyped image that make Fès the spiritual and cultural capital of the kingdom, Rabat the political and university capital and Marrakech pearl of the south and tourist capital, reveal a basic injustice with regard to the "Ismailia city" left in a corner with her agricultural-food-producing role.

The unmistakable Bab el-Mansour, the most important gate
in the walls of Meknès.

Meknès is suffering from an incomprehensible dead-calm in tourism to the extent that fortune and growth in one field can overshadow another causing weakness and pallor. And yet, these two sectors (agriculture and tourism) have proved complementary in other places and have become more and more unified" (from the "Tribune de Meknès").

There is no other way of explaining why all the attractions of the region have been shifted to the background and it has not been possible to launch a resolute project for developing tourism. We cannot passively accept the role attributed to Meknès on the relative chessboard of Morocco, and it is definitely inappropriate in relation to its heritage that the city of Moulay Ismail not be able to take its rightful place on the circuit of the imperial cities.

Situated in a position similar to that of nearby Fès, Meknès enjoys the same advantages: crossroads of the east-west and north-south routes, it has enormous agricultural potential and an abundant water supply. But, as opposed to what occurred in Fès, here the richness of the farming lands cast a shadow on the city's and region's other potentials. And, if that were not sufficient, all around Meknès sites and ruins can be the starting point

for excursions that will instruct the mind and refresh the sprit: Volubilis and Moulay Idris are just two examples. The hills of the Rif extend an invitation to discover a countryside which, from springtime on is dressed in the magnificent, myriad hued robes of the local flora. For some years now, clever promoters have been organizing horseback excursions to discover the natural environment and come into contact with the local population. The Moyen Atlas is very close to Meknès: it can be reached via Ifrane or Azroue. The second route also provides an opportunity for admiring one of the most amazing landscapes in the entire Moyen Atlas, at **Ito**. Just before Azrou, a natural terrace opens over a valley spiked with hills, an almost lunar landscape that is testimony of the region's volcanic origins.

However, it does indeed seem that Meknès plans on basing its development mainly on agriculture. That the area is rich and the agricultural potential enormous are undeniable. Furthermore, abundant crop yield has made it possible to create an important food-processing industry, while the Meknès olive groves are so famous throughout the country that the city ranks second as far as the number of olive-pressing plants are concerned, and is home to one of the largest olive-oil plants in all Morocco. Grape growing has also developed significantly, and the local wine-makers turn out excellent wines such as *Toulal* and *Guerrouane*. In any event, the various industrial plants have not succeeded in creating a solid base, so that Meknès is still far from the country's main industrial cities, with only 25% of its population engaged in the so-called "secondary" sector.

Like the other inland imperial cities, Meknès, which in 1994 had a population of roughly five hundred thousand, has had moderate demographic growth. In the 'sixties the geographers, Depois and Raynal defined it as a city of "farmers and soldiers" and even today, notwithstanding the great impact that industry and tourism have had on the area and the socio-economic panorama, contributing to strengthening the city-element, it has not shrugged off this image. The city is fully open to the country, especially the many peripheral "developments" that have been absorbed within the recently redefined urban perimeter.

Taking advantage of the implementation of a general recovery plan, various city leaders are joining forces to improve the appearance of Meknès, and provide it with mainly culturally oriented entertainment facilities. An exhibition gallery has been established at Bab el-Mansour and an ambitious project is underway to transform the immediate surroundings of Sahrij es-Souani into an out-

The decorations on Bab el-Mansour consist of arabesques of rosettes, stars and broken lines, while the short marble pillars support the arches flanked by slender columns with Corinthian capitals.

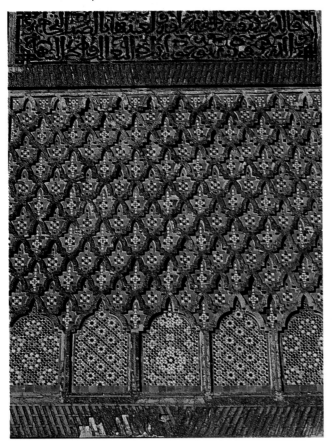

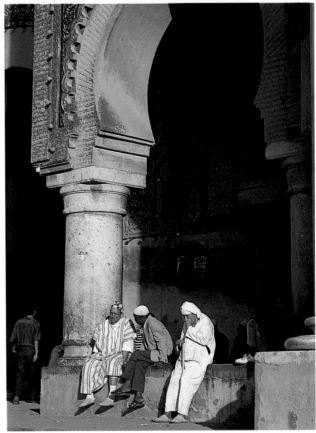

The impressive Bab el-Khémis leads to the old mellah and gardens.

door recreation area that can give the people of Meknès an oasis of greenery worthy of the monuments that surround the basin. Yet another project focuses on salvaging one of the city's most prestigious libraries, that is the library in the Great Mosque. And what a wonderful idea, to place the new library in a building that has also been saved from total neglect. A traditional home, built at the beginning of the XX century, has already been designated as the new library. Now, Dar el-Bachaouat, the former residence of the pasha of Meknès, in the heart of the old city, will offer its salons, and its *riad*, the stupendous garden, to all those who cannot remain indifferent to the heritage of the "Ismailia city".

From the urbanistic standpoint, Meknès is divided into three distinct sectors: the new city, child of the protectorate that dates from the beginning of the XX century, on the right bank of the Wadi Bou Fekrane; and the two older sections on the left bank. The first, on the north is the old nucleus within the walls, the medina: it is the original city, modified and embellished by the Marinids and the 'Alawis. It was the Marinid, Abou Inan who built the Abou Inania Madrasah, during the same era as the madrasah of Fès. Moulay Ismail built the Bab el-Khémis and Bab el-Bardayn gates of the mosque of the same name and the Jewish quarter.

The imperial city

The **imperial city** with all its annexes was built, by Moulay Ismail south of the medina. It is a group of buildings separated by gardens. To the north-east rises **Dar Kebira**, south of which Moulay Ismail built another group of palaces known as **Dar el-Makhzen**. Between Bab el-Khémis and Dar Kebira there was another district for government officials. The city was also flanked by a series of annexes used as quarters for the troops and as warehouses: the Kasba Hedrache, the stables, the granaries and the Agdal basin.

The imperial city was protected by *pisé* fortified walls, that were truly impressive since they extended over 40 kilometers with all the fortifications; the bastions alone were 25 km. But, in some places there were actually three different sized walls to defend the city: the first was about as high a man standing and seems to have served for stopping horsemen, so that only the most obstinate foot

The smallest, typically horseshoe shaped gate, Bab Jama el-Nouar is not far from Bab el-Mansour.

The mighty fortifications that surround the city of Meknès are now flanked by plazas and gardens. On the left, the wide Bab el-Bardayn that leads into the mosque of the same name.

soldiers could get through. Those who did pass the first obstacle were usually stopped at the second, much more powerful walls: only agile, tenacious young attackers could tackle the second bastion to be met by a colossal wall of enormous height. This wall served not only to defend the imperial city, it was also a trap for those, who reached it after expending enormous amounts of energy. Already worn out, they could not continue their attack, nor could they turn back! It was a system for getting the enemy with its back literally to the wall.

Inside the palace everything was created to permit absolute autonomy, thereby avoiding any direct dependence on the outside if the hordes of horsemen from the Atlas and Rif reached the Sais plain and tried to besiege the capital. Granaries, stables that could probably house up to twelve thousand horses, irrigation pools and wells runs by norias reveal, even today, the perfect military and economic organization of the site.

Thus, if Fès is famous for its houses and fabulous palaces, for its madrasahs and sumptuous mosque-universities, Meknès is known for it s fortresses, the impres-

sive clay buildings, and mainly for its "bab", the richly decorated monumental gates.

One of these gates deserves particular mention, **Bab el-Mansour el-Aleuj,** the "Gate of the Victorious Renegade" that gets its name from the architect who built it, a Christian convert to Islam. Pierre Loti left a highly detailed description that reveals the underlying concept and the decorative apparatus: "The gate... is a gigantic ogive, supported by marble pillars and framed by elegant festoons. The entire wall... is covered with fine, majolica mosaics, as complex as fine embroideries. The two square bastions that flank this gate on the right and left, are also covered with similar mosaics and also rest on marble pillars. Rosettes, stars and endless arabesques, unimaginable geometric combinations that intrigue the eye like a riddle while attesting to the finest and most original taste, have been accumulated here with myriad bits of enameled clay, now concave, now convex creating, from afar, the illusion of a priceless woven brocade that sparkles and glimmers as if it were stretched across these old stones to break up the monotony of the tall bastions."

The entrance to Dar Jamai, today the Museum of Moroccan Art.

The next gate is **Bab el-Khémis**, monumental, less elaborately decorated than the preceding one but no less fascinating. In fact, although only the rectangle that frames the gate with the arch over the entrance is decorated, Bab el-Khémis does have something fascinating, that sensation of paradox deriving perhaps from the subtly rich decoration or the elegance of the polychrome geometric motifs on a powerful clay wall that strike the eye like an oasis in a dull space. Curved ornaments frame a horseshoe arch of black, angular stones surrounded by *zellij* in a shade of green that once must have been brilliant, but now has been muted by time.

Certainly, the other gates also deserve a look even if they are less impressive than the two we just described. One is **Bab el-Bardayn** that gets its name from the pack-animal market (mules and donkeys) that is held nearby. Beyond the gate, next to the cemetery there is a green-roofed mausoleum. It is the **Sanctuary of Sidi Mohammed ben Aissa**, known as Cheikh el-Kamel, founder of the

Confraternity of the Aissaoua. This mystic, who was probâbly born among the Bou Sbaa and lived between the end of the XV and early XVI centuries is the protagonist of an entire body of legends. A follower of the Tarika el-Jazoulia, before he moved permanently to Meknès he frequented the most eminent *imams* of Marrakech and Fès. His powerful confraternity spread through Morocco and extended to the Middle East. Members of this order gather every weekend in the Mausoleum of Sidi Mohammed ben Aissa; the ceremony that begins after the *el-Asr* prayers, the third of the day, lasts late into evening. The neighborhoods near the sanctuary resound with the songs of the large crowd that gathers to attend to participate in the ceremony known as *hadra*, led by the *mokkadem* the group's spiritual leader, and enlivened by the sounds of *bendir* (drums), *tarija* (tambourines) and *ghayta* (oboes). During the ceremony the members of the confraternity sing chants, the men stand and the women sit - aside from those who fall into a trance. The ceremony be-

64

The interior of the museum where we can admire authentic masterpieces of the artistic crafts from the city and the entire country

gins with slow rhythms, that gradually accelerate to the point that the dancers go into a form of trance that allows them to perform the most amazing steps.

The *moussem* of Sidi Mohammed ben Aissa takes place on the occasion of the *mouloud*. At this time Meknès is transformed into gathering place of the Aissaoua who come from all parts of Morocco. The celebrations last for seven days during which the area around the mausoleum looks like a tent-city.

Bab er-Rih, or the "Gate of the Wind" opens onto a long corridor that captures the *chergui* (the east wind that corresponds to the mistral or sirocco); the gusts along the corridor are so strong that they will literally sweep away anything in their path. Located to the right of Bâb el-Mansour el-Aleuf, **Bab Jamaa en-Nouara** (The "Gate of the Mosque of Flowers") looks like a modest door, but it gives the visitor sensation of rediscovering a more harmonious and human dimension.

At this point, we can enter the bastions for a recog-

The flourishing gardens of Dar Jamai.

nizance tour that will start with the **Mosque-Mausoleum of Moulay Ismail**. Anyone can enter this place, even non-Muslims, as long as they remove their shoes. The entrance is via the *Bab Moulay Ismail* door, that is less lavishly decorated than those opening to the outside. It is still beautiful however, with a foiled ogival arch, the carved and gilded sandstone edges and protected by a neo-classical canopy. The first room with the customary marble fountain is covered by a painted wooden roof. Then, we cross several rooms that are open to the sky where we can admire a remarkably accurate solar *clock* on the north wall. Before we reach the tomb chamber we go through a square room with a dome and twelve, highly elegant marble columns that probably come from Volubilis. The *tomb* of the founder of imperial Meknès is carved from white marble and is surrounded by the tombs of two of his children and one of his wives. Two *clocks*, gifts of Louis XIV watch over the eternal rest of the sovereign's soul. Thanks to recent, and highly skilled restorations, the entire complex is in excellent condition. As we leave the mausoleum we enter a corridor which, after 2 kilometers brings us east to a series of enormous buildings.

The granaries of Moulay Ismail (or **Héri es-Souani**), **Dar el-Mar** (the "Palace of the Water"), and **Sahrij es Souani** (the pool of the Agdal) located to the south, not far from the mausoleum form a vast complex which even today emanates that almost obsessive quest for security that distinguished the second 'Alawi sovereign. From this we can perhaps understand why the Ottomans never tried to establish their domination over the Ismailian kingdom and considered Morocco a respected or feared neighbor.

The granaries, or what is left of them, are a true labyrinth of arches and naves (there are twenty-three). Even though the definition of granary is the most common, it has never been historically proved that this building was ever really used to store cereals. Some speak of stables other of armories. It matters little, the ruins of the original structure serve their purpose as a photogenic point for souvenir collectors.

North of Dar el-Ma and the granaries there is a large pool of water that was once used to irrigate the palace gardens and to amuse the royal family and its entourage.

Even such a brief visit, however, cannot be considered complete without going down into the large and impressive cellars of the **Cara prison** named for the architect who built it. He was a Portuguese captive who is believed to have designed the prison in exchange for freedom after having received an explicit promise of liberation from Moulay Ismail. In this case too, there is no real proof that it was ever really a prison. According to some sources this immense, vaulted underground room that is 14 kilometers wide may have be used for storing grain.

During protectorate, two Frenchman who went to explore this vast cellar, with only a dog as their guide were lost and never returned. It was immediately decided to close off much of the labyrinth, leaving only the part near the entrance door open to visitors.

After we leave the underground chamber, we should stop at the **Koubat el-Khayatin** (the "Dome of the Tailors").

A bustling street in Meknès.

The courtyard of the Bou Inania Madrasah;
the extraordinarily rich decorations resemble
a brocade fabric.

It was here that Moulay Ismail received foreign guests
and emissaries who came to settle political questions or
obtain the release of their compatriots.

We go through Bab el-Mansour and then it is worthwhile
to look around the **medina** of Meknès. A *souk* consisting
of covered and outdoor stalls flanks the *kaysarie* and the
business streets. It provides a fine opportunity for becom-
ing acquainted with the local crafts and the regional
products that are peculiar to the city. There is even a museum dedicated entirely to the crafts of Meknès where we
can see the finest examples of this artistic heritage: textiles, embroideries, terra-cottas, pottery, damasks, wrought
iron, jewelry, carved wood and clothing. The **Museum of
Dar Jamai** (Jamai Palace) named for the founder of this
nineteenth century middle class home offers a complete
overview of the city's and region's artistic crafts.

A madrasah, **Bou Inania** named for the indefatigable
Marinid builder of this type of structure, Abou Inan,

The typical, colorful ceramic and stucco work decorations where floral and geometric motifs intertwine with cursive and Kufic inscriptions.

dates from the XIV century. In shape and concept it is a perfect reflection of the canons and models in vogue for this type of edifice between the XIII and XIV centuries. Here we can see all the motifs and components that we found in its "sisters" in Fès, they may have been made less skillfully simply because at the time Meknès had not attained the rank of capital. But there is the same spiritual fervor: internal courtyard, carved wood, carved stucco, glazed majolica, ornamental or protective roofs and green tiles.

Therefore, it should not come as a surprise to learn that, in the mid-nineties, Meknès obtained well-deserved recognition as part of the world heritage from UNESCO.

Men and women dressed in their usual colorful costumes crowd the streets of Meknès day after day.

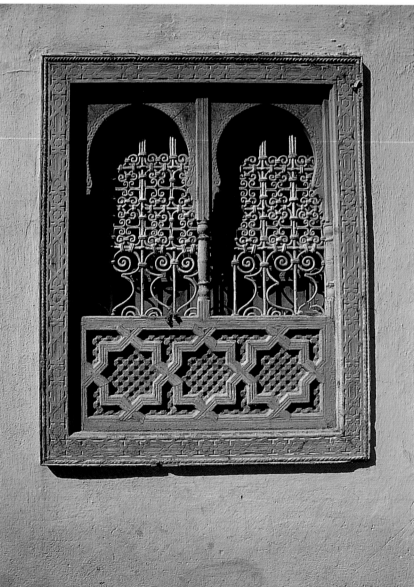

*Even doors and windows are works of art in Meknès.
Even the locks are typical products of Morocco.*

A broad, paved street leads to the House of Orpheus.

VOLUBILIS

At the foot of Jebel Zerhoun the two cities, Roman Volubilis and Idrisid Moulay Idris de Zerhoun symbolized the alternation and coexistence of cultures and civilizations in Morocco. The "dead city" and the "living city" require that the visitor touring the imperial cities take a slight, yet totally worthwhile detour. From the features of the places that were chosen to build the two cities we can clearly see the political situations and social conditions, like the founders' economic relations and contributions, with respect to their regional context in the broadest sense. It was a context that was both liberal and closed, it was dominated by a Berber community hostile to any foreigners entering their territory.

A quick geo-strategic reading of the locations of the extinct city (Volubilis) and the holy city (Moulay Idris) allows us to present a contextual "explanation-interpretation."

For Moulay Idris de Zerhoun the choice of site depended directly on the shortage of weapons and the weakness of the armies called upon to defend the young dynasty and the new religion, Islam that the *sharif* wanted to propagate. Thus it was necessary to seek support and protection on a rocky spur to ward off any surprise attacks. Faith was the main weapon of Idris I founder of the city that bears his name and of the first Muslim kingdom in Morocco (VIII century). It was a faith that his followers and allies, through exhortation and preaching, managed to spread through a socio-tribal system based on a primarily oral cultural tradition, a conglomerate of confeder-

*Here, and on the following pages: the splendid ruins
of the House of Orpheus, with its incredibly colored mosaics
depicting mythological subjects or scenes from daily life.*

ated tribes that ferociously opposed any domination imposed by force.

Volubilis, the Roman city based its existence on a much more concrete defensive structure. Strong and secure because of its military power, the city used a totally avant-garde technique to conquer and subjugate the surrounding areas that attracted it for reasons of security and/or interest. The famous *limes*, the Roman road was a line of demarcation in a certain sense. Then, in a valorous effort, the city felt a need, as it were, to show off its architectural greatness and its urbanistic majesty to defend these human, economic and territorial acquisitions. It is obvious

that being so advanced with respect to the rudimentary methods of the ancient Berbers assured Volubilis its supremacy. It is also important to remember that the city was first established in 40 BC.

Situated at 34°4'30" north and 5°33'30" west, Volubilis was truly an avant-garde city. The reasonable distance between it and the plains of Gharb and Sais allowed its inhabitants to satisfy their needs for agricultural products. The strategic proximity of the Atlas mountains and the Rif also guaranteed defensibility from the military standpoint and the possibility of organizing expeditions to these mountains to get cedar wood, fur bearing ani-

The ruins of the Capitol, with the elegant staircase and slender columns.

mals, or game. Some mosaics that have survived to the present, such as those in the House of Orpheus, provide amazing documentation about the fauna of the period.

The Roman ruins stand on a plateau characterized by a slight south-west slope. According to the archeologists, it was inhabited as early as the Neolithic period, and was occupied by the Carthaginians prior to the arrival of the Romans. In the III century the Berbers took over from the Romans occupying the city until the IX century when, for reasons that are still a mystery, they left, leaving the city intact. Perhaps it was because of the inroads being made by Islam, or rather the birth of Fès? Thus, for eight centuries this jewel of Roman civilization continued to display its buildings and splendid mosaics as if nothing had happened; no one dared to penetrate it as if a curse had been cast over the ghost city. The curse did, in fact, seem to materialize in the disastrous earthquake that struck Lisbon in 1755 and the pillage that followed it. The city seemed to sink into the ground, as if to save what was still salvageable, and remained there until Tissot discovered the ruins in 1874.

Although the first excavations were begun in 1887, the world had to wait until the mid-nineteen twenties to learn about the secrets of Roman Volubilis, when the mighty fortifications were unearthed. The place that is currently the "cemetery" of the ruins of the ancient settlement of

Above, the Capitol.
Below and to the right, some of the splendid mosaics that adorn the buildings in Volubilis.

The majestic ruins of the Basilica, the place were justice was administered during the Roman period.

Volubilis is surrounded by bastions that measure from 1.5 to 1.8 meters in thickness. Since not a single part of the walls still stands at its original height, it has been estimated that they may have reached as high as 5-6 meters. The walls, that ran in a polygon for 2.35 km seem to have had forty bastions and eight gates. They protected the ancient city during the period of its greatest splendor extended over 40 hectares and was home to about twelve thousand people.

Even today, when the visitor to Volubilis passes through the three districts that comprise the city, it is easy to understand how rationally it was designed. In the southeast section a rather small district extends to a hill that overlooks the Wadi Kroumane that is crossed by a little bridge. This district, with its many oil presses and some luxurious homes decorated with mosaics is now the entrance to the archeological site.

About 200 meters north of the first district, in the middle of the ancient settlement are the ruins of what was the heart of the city's public and administrative life. Here we can see the forum, the capitol and slightly further on, the Arch of Triumph built to honor Caracalla. These prestigious buildings circumscribe a central area between the ancient city (in the south-east) and the residential districts to the north-east which the archeologists define as the "Roman quarters".

The ruins of the forum, the capitol and the basilica show us how well they used their construction materials to achieve extraordinary harmony between the topography and the buildings. The whole appears urbanistically and architecturally well-structured, with skill and expertise unusual for a Roman city located so far inland.

For those who are content with a brief, amateur-style visit there are at least twelve important places not to miss. We can start with the one closest to the entrance. The **House of Orpheus** is famous for its mosaic in which the artists used the entire range of colors that can be created with just three materials: marble, terra-cotta and glass paste. A perfectly conserved medallion depicts the wild game of ancient Morocco with astounding realism.

The Arch of Triumph, built to honor Caracalla in 217.

The **Forum** consists of a small (1300 square meters), paved square. It is likely that the statues that decorated the outer perimeter (as the enormous stone blocks that must have been the pedestals, that are still aligned around it lead us to believe) that they were taken to Rome in a great hurry.

The **Basilica**, or as the historians prefer to call it, the Civil Basilica, was the place where justice was administered during the Roman era. A staircase of stone blocks runs along the façade and leads to three doors topped by ogival arches. The interior has three naves with two rows of columns with Corinthian capitals. When the excavations were begun, the Basilica and the Arch of Triumph were the only two monuments that still towered over the mass of buried ruins.

The **Capitol**, or rather, the building identified as the capitol on the basis of an inscription dedicated to the emperor Macrinus in 217 AD is located south of the Basilica. It has a large door that connects with the Forum. The height and shape of the building can be hypothesized on the basis of the columns that were reconstructed using pieces found on the site.

The **Arch of Triumph** also dates from 217: erected in honor of Caracalla it opens onto the main road, the *Decumanus Maximus* and dominates the fertile plains below to the west of the site. The powerful arch, built of mainly dark-grey stone blocks still bears some of the elegant decorations on the face: partly reconstructed inscriptions, medallions and small columns.

The **House of the Ephebus** has a fine mosaic in the *triclinium* or dining room. The decoration is characterized by lively colors and interesting patters. The house itself contains ten (two unfortunately were lost) medallions that superbly depict the twelve labors of Hercules.

To the north, a splendid district runs on either side of the *Decumanus Maximus*, the ancestor of today's broad avenues, that crosses the city from north to south without any curves or interruption, displaying all its majesty between the Arch of Triumph and the Tangier Gate. It is evenly paved and was the main road, along which the most luxurious homes once stood. There is no doubt that this was the aristocratic district: it is sufficient to see just how many private residences flank the *Decumanus*. The progressive unsettling of the ground caused the paving stones to slip, so in many cases they no longer touch, but we can still see the incredibly well-engineered water drainage channel that ran in the middle of the road.

A mosaic entitled "Of the Four Seasons" decorates the **House of Dionysius**. The manner in which these masterpieces were decorated, conceived and made leads us to believe that they were inspired by a range of styles that had been codified in Rome.

The **House of the Cortege of Venus** has yielded valuable and information and treasures to the archeologists: a mosaic floor that extends through eight rooms and seven corridors, the famous bust of Juba II and other masterpieces of Roman art which are now in the Rabat Archeological Museum or the Tangier Museum.

We reach the **Capitol** via a broad, even staircase of cut stone blocks. It leads directly to what must have been the court of justice where Roman "high-society" also met. On the southern part, with the exception of the mosaics, the way the stones are cut and sculpted is rather amateurish, as opposed to the Forum where the cut stones alone represent the apogee of Roman art in Morocco. The use of these large stones, directly juxtaposed without any breaks in either the literal or figurative sense, reveal fascinating art and great skill. The elegance that must have distinguished society in the city is indisputably obvious in the

The elegant ruins of the building known as the House of the Columns.

The airy House of the Cortege of Venus.

Left, the straight Decumanus Maximus that led to the Arch of Triumph is flanked by the ruins of the Forum.

structure and decorative apparatus of the middle class homes. The ruins of the contoured, fluted or twisted columns, made with extreme care leave no doubt that Rome considered this place the capital of Mauretania Tingitana. Only time has managed to cloud the nobility of the materials, the rationality of the organization and the harmony of the creations. And, notwithstanding the lack of an amphitheater, the amazing level of urban life can be understood from the finely sculpted monuments, the creative talents behind the works of art and the decorative opulence of the mosaics. In parallel, as we walk among the ruins, we cannot help but think of the difficult lives of the slaves and captives who labored in the construction sites of Volubilis. But then, is it legitimate to criticize a Roman Empire that was obsessed primarily by the desire to dominate the Mediterranean world through force and intimidation? Recourse to exploitation and refined gigantism was the most appropriate way of consolidating dominion of an empire that was the carrier and propagator of a civilization committed first to domination through power and then to convincing the world through the exercise of power of what it was able to achieve.

MOULAY IDRIS

Moulay Idris de Zerhoun site of the Mausoleum of Moulay Idris el-Akbar, father of Moulay Idris el-Azhar who is buried in Fès, is a holy city, built into the slopes of the Zerhoun massif with a population of approximately thirteen thousand. The Zerhoun is part of what is usually known as the Pré-Rif: it is a group of low mountains and hills of clay and marl, an unstable combination that comprises the piedmont of the Rif. The entire region is dedicated to traditional agriculture based on grains and trees. It is also a land of olive groves that extend over most of the high ground, while the landscape is dotted with hillside villages.

The holy city of Moulay Idris enjoys an extraordinary position of rolling hills. Two of these hills that are part of the massif have the same names as the two main districts, Khiber and Tasga and divide the town. For those who first see the city from above, it is a breathtaking spectacle with the cascade of houses and a tangle of terraces that seem to rest on each other. This mass of cubes is broken only by the outlines of the **Mausoleum of Moulay Idris**, with its sloping, green tiled roofs.

The Khiber district, in the upper part of the city offers one of the best observation points: from a terrace near the Mosque of Sidi Abd Allah el-Hajjam, we can look almost straight down to see the entire settlement. Before reaching the terrace we will see one of the true curiosities of Moulay Idris, one of the few cylindrical minarets in Morocco, with the date of construction 1939, clearly visible. It appears completely covered with green tiles which in Kufic script read "There is no God but Allah and Mohammed is His prophet."

One of the greatest *moussem* in all Morocco is held every year - in August or September to honor the founder of the city and of the first Moroccan dynasty. Pilgrims come to

Views of the holy city of Moulay Idris on the slopes of Zerhoun, and the unmistakable outlines of the Mausoleum.

Moulay Idris from the most distant parts of the country bringing their offerings in the hope of receiving the *baraka*, the blessing of the *sharif*, direct descendant of the Prophet. On this occasion we can see impressive groupings of tents and the *fantasie*, traditional equestrian exhibitions are organized. But the special moment of the *moussem* is the recital of verses from the Koran while the main *moussamiyn* of the kingdom gather to sing religious chants known as *amdahs*.

Left, the original architecture and fine green ceramic covering of one of the few cylindrical minarets in Morocco can be seen at Moulay Idris; below, the city's streets and souk.

IFRANE

Even though from afar the roofs seem to be covered with red tiles, we are not in the Alps. When they built this mountain town in the nineteen twenties, the founders of **Ifrane** must have drawn their inspiration from European alpine villages. The position is ideal: slightly over 1600 meters above sea level, and the city benefits from an extraordinary environmental setting that is perfect for rest and restoring calm and tranquillity. The air is pure, thanks to the nearby forests, the greenery rests the eye and the soft rustle of the waters calms the spirit.

Its high altitude makes Ifrane equally inviting in winter and summer, as it only changes its attire to give each season a special look. When dressed in white it draws winter sports enthusiasts: the nearby slopes of Mischliffen or Jebel Hébri offer facilities for skiing and sledding, and all the equipment can be found in the town. In summer Ifrane is a wonderful vacation place, a favorite for weekends or longer periods, with many chalets and villas available for tourists.

The town has managed to preserve its quiet, tranquil character. It is well organized with well-kept roads. Even the streets and green areas are well planned with an eye to environmental impact. In a certain way Ifrane recalls those cities where exotic plants enhance the atmosphere with their fragrances and colors.

When arriving from Fès or Meknès the sight of the forest means that Ifrane is close at hand. In fact, from the time we leave the Sais plain to see the first spurs of the Moyen Atlas, our attention is captured by the vast forests. Here, in the Moyen Atlas we find the most beautiful forest in all Morocco, and Ifrane has the best conserved cedar forest. The cedar is a splendid tree, that grows to majestic heights, as tall as forty meters, pushing the sky. It changes appearance with age: when young it has a pointed peak, like an arrow aimed at the clouds; with the weight of the years its top spreads and widens into a fascinating sight. These trees can live for a very long time, such as the **Gouraud cedar** near Azrou that has a circumference of over 7 meters. It was probably planted in the same period, during the XIII century, that the Marinids founded Fès el-Jédid. Cedar wood, that has always been widely used in construction, is found in nearly all of the ancient buildings in Fès: madrasahs, mosques, palaces, etc.

In contrast to the heat that reigns on the Sais plain and

A panoramic view of Ifrane, with houses nestled amidst the vegetation is reminiscent of the Alps.

The most beautiful cedar forests in Morocco are located near Ifrane, in the incredible environmental context of the Moyen Atlas. The Gouraud cedar (right) enjoys fame of its own because of its age: over seven hundred years.

its villages, the fresh air of high altitude and the abundance of water make the area around Ifrane seem like a paradise. The water collects in a series of basins known as *daiets* or *aguelmanes* that have made the entire area famous, and draw people from afar: fishing enthusiasts and those who merely want to relax. These lakes, that vary in size, from 4 to 150 hectares, make for an interesting tour starting from Ifrane itself. Naturally, there are some stretches that may pose some problems especially in winter, but the scenery with its beautiful landscapes, and the jewel-like lakes, certainly makes the effort worthwhile. The gently waving hills, the steep, forest-covered escarpments, calcareous rock deposits, green meadows and fields of lavender that reach as far as the eye can see, the conifer and oak forests, come together with the features peculiar to a karstic landscape.

Now a provincial capital Ifrane is making considerable efforts to meet the responsibilities of its role. It has already become the seat of prestigious institutions, the most recent of which is the **El-Akhawayn University** that opened its doors in 1995. This is the only institute of higher learning in North Africa where English is taught. The campus extends over an area of about 50 hectares and has thirty-seven pavilion-shaped buildings with sloping, red-tiled roofs.

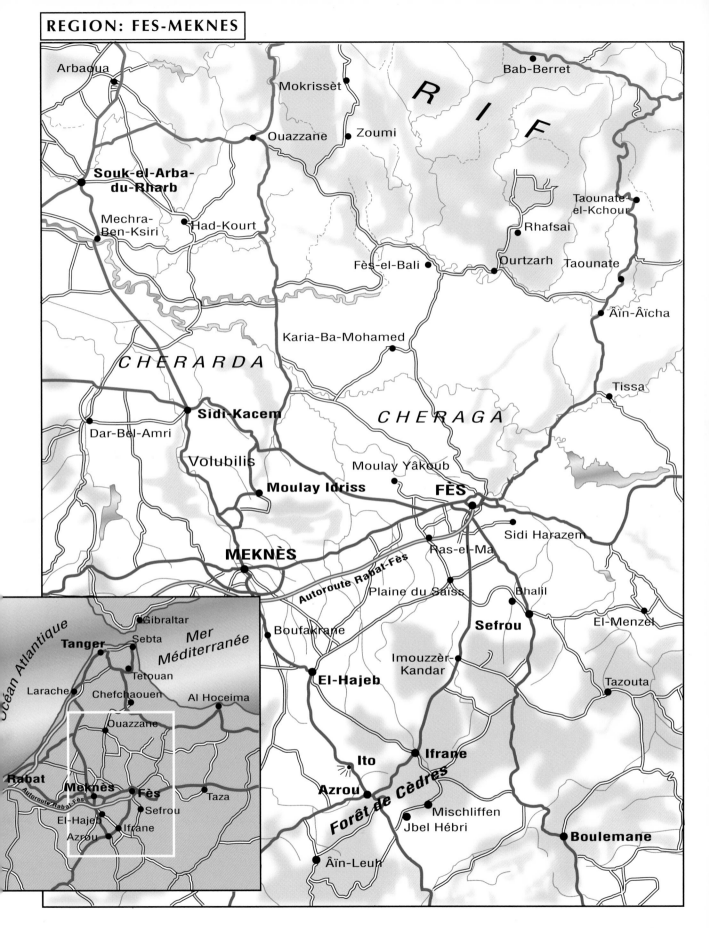

REGION: FES-MEKNES

Arbaoua

Mokrissèt

Bab-Berret

R I F

Ouazzane · Zoumi

Souk-el-Arba-du-Rharb

Taounate-el-Kchour

Mechra-Ben-Ksiri · Had-Kourt

Rhafsai

Fès-el-Bali · Ourtzarh · Taounate

Âïn-Âïcha

Karia-Ba-Mohamed

C H E R A R D A

Tissa

Sidi-Kacem

C H E R A G A

Dar-Bel-Amri

Volubilis

Moulay Yâkoub

Moulay Idriss

FÈS

Sidi Harazem

MEKNÈS

Ras-el-Ma

Autoroute Rabat-Fès

Plaine du Saïss

Bhalil

El-Menzel

Boufakrane

Sefrou

El-Hajeb

Imouzzèr-Kandar

Tazouta

Ito · Ifrane

Azrou · Forêt de Cèdres

Mischliffen

Boulemane

Jbel Hébri

Âïn-Leuh

Océan Atlantique

Gibraltar

Mer Méditerranée

Tanger · Sebta

Tetouan

Larache · Chefchaouen · Al Hoceima

Ouazzane

Rabat

Meknès · Fès · Taza

Autoroute Rabat-Fès

Sefrou

El-Hajeb · Ifrane

Azrou

INDEX